GALAXY OF SUPERSTARS

CHELSEA HOUSE PUBLISHERS

GALAXY OF SUPERSTARS

Ewan McGregor

Veda Boyd Jones

CHELSEA HOUSE PUBLISHERS
Philadelphia

Frontis: *Ewan McGregor, who was successful in many European independent films before being cast as Obi-Wan Kenobi in* Star Wars: Episode I—The Phantom Menace. *Despite the fame that his latest role has brought, Ewan stays grounded and hasn't forgotten his small-town Scottish roots.*

Produced by
21st Century Publishing and Communications, Inc.
New York, New York
http://www.21cpc.com

CHELSEA HOUSE PUBLISHERS

Editor in Chief: Stephen Reginald
Managing Editor: James D. Gallagher
Production Manager: Pamela Loos
Art Director: Sara Davis
Director of Photography: Judy L. Hasday
Senior Production Editor: LeeAnne Gelletly
Publishing Coordinator/Project Editor: James McAvoy
Assistant Editor: Anne Hill
Cover Designer: Emiliano Begnardi

Front Cover Photo: Denis Van Tine/London Features Int'l
Back Cover Photo: Miramax Films/Photofest

The Chelsea House World Wide Web address is
http://www.chelseahouse.com

First Printing

1 3 5 7 9 8 6 4 2

Library of Congress Cataloging-in-Publication Data

Jones, Veda Boyd.
    Ewan McGregor / Veda Boyd Jones.
    p. cm.— (Galaxy of superstars)
    Includes bibliographical references and index.
Summary: A biography of the Scottish-born actor who has become well-known in the United States because of his role in the recent popular movie, Star Wars: Episode I—The Phantom Menace.
        ISBN 0-7910-5501-9 — ISBN 0-7910-5502-7 (pbk.)
1. McGregor, Ewan, 1971—Juvenile literature. 2. Motion picture actors and actresses—Scotland—Biography—Juvenile literature. [1. McGregor, Ewan, 1971-2.Actors and actresses.] I. Title. II. Series.
PN2604.M38 J66 1999
791.43'028'092—dc21
    [B]   99-052500
                                                                              CIP
                                                                               AC

CONTENTS

1

THE FORCE IS WITH HIM

Scottish actor Ewan McGregor was decked out in a blond wig, tight snakeskin pants, and platform shoes for his role as a rock star in a "glitter-rock" movie when his cell phone rang. The director yelled "cut," and Ewan took the call from his agent, Lindy King.

He could barely understand her words as her voice shrilled with excitement. This was it. *The* call had come. Ewan would play the young Obi-Wan Kenobi in episode one of the new *Star Wars* prequels. But he was sworn to secrecy.

Ewan hung up the phone on that March day in 1997. This would be the biggest film of his life and he couldn't say a word. He tried to concentrate on his current role.

"I had to walk around knowing I got the part and not being able to tell anyone. It was quite hard."

Of course, he couldn't keep the news to himself. "I told my wife . . . and my parents, and that was it. I didn't tell anyone else for a long while."

For over a year, the press had speculated about who *Star Wars* creator George Lucas would cast as the most

---

Ewan McGregor as the young Obi-Wan Kenobi in Star Wars: Episode I—The Phantom Menace. *As a boy, Ewan had loved the original* Star Wars *movies. Preparing for his role, he said, "I've been waiting 20 years to have my own light saber."*

beloved Jedi knight. Even after Ewan had received the call, movie personnel misled the media by saying Ewan was one of several actors being considered for the role of Obi-Wan. The intent was to release the names of the entire cast at one time.

But Ewan was too eager. "What I've been told to say," he confided to a reporter for *Entertainment Weekly* in June, "is that we're in negotiations. But the truth is, I want to do it, they want me to do it, so I'm doing it."

The leak was big news. Later, *Star Wars* producer Rick McCallum confirmed that Ewan had the part. McCallum called Ewan a real chameleon for his ability to take on a wide variety of movie roles. "He is really a mercurial, multitalented, multifaceted human being."

Many of the great hordes of *Star Wars* fans questioned the wisdom of the choice. Although Ewan McGregor had been in an American film, he was not a household name in the United States. He was well-known only in Britain and Europe for his roles in independent films. Ewan had been in movies where he had appeared nude. He'd played parts from a gay rocker to a heroin addict. He was outspoken, swore profusely, drank lots of beer, and chain-smoked. He was not a role model for children, and the scope of the *Star Wars* prequel would have millions of kids idolizing him.

George Lucas explained why he chose the Scottish actor to play the part that another distinguished actor, Sir Alec Guinness, had made famous in the earlier *Star Wars* trilogy. "Ewan is witty, enthusiastic, and impatient. These are qualities of Obi-Wan. I'm always looking for actors whose own personality will emerge and enrich the characters they play."

George Lucas, the creator of the Star Wars *films. Lucas explained his choice of Ewan for the younger version of the character played by Sir Alec Guinness in the original* Star Wars *movie. He said that Ewan, like Obi-Wan Kenobi, is "witty, enthusiastic, and impatient."*

Fans accepted Lucas's reasoning, but Ewan kept a fairly low profile before the release of the movie. Other *Star Wars* actors made the talk show circuit, but not Ewan. Still, his character graced many magazine covers. Select magazines, including *Vanity Fair* and *GQ*, whose readers would appreciate the unself-conscious Ewan, featured frank interviews with the actor instead of merely printing publicity biographies.

Star Wars: Episode I—The Phantom Menace goes back in time to a galaxy far, far away to explain events that led up to the original trilogy. The fourth episode, *A New Hope*, was released in 1977. Episode V, *The Empire Strikes Back*, fascinated moviegoers in 1980, and the sixth installment, *The Return of the Jedi*, hypnotized fans in 1983.

Sixteen years had passed since the last episode, and *Star Wars* had developed a somewhat cult-like following, including Ewan, who had watched each of the films countless times. Although the trilogy had been available on video for years, they were updated in 1997 with sound and image enhancement and re-released to the big screen for a new generation. Now more people than ever were hyped about the release of the first prequel.

The original *Star Wars* was one of the first movies to have a huge marketing campaign tied to it. Action figures of the characters were sold. T-shirts, lunch boxes, and backpacks sported the *Star Wars* logo. As a kid, even Ewan slept on *Star Wars* sheets and spent hours sparring with his brother and friends with his *Star Wars* light saber.

The publicity for the film escalated as the opening date neared. Lucas moved the date forward two days from May 21 to May 19, 1999. Die-hard fans camped outside theaters for weeks before advance tickets went on sale. Some fans wore special prequel camp-out T-shirts. Other campers turned their stays into charity events with sponsors paying for each hour that fans waited in line.

At one minute after midnight on Monday, May 3, toy stores across the nation opened to sell the new *Star Wars* toys. Of course, the new four-inch Obi-Wan Kenobi figure looked like Ewan McGregor.

Back at the theater lines, sidewalks were covered with more tents, sleeping bags, and even a couch or two. *Star Wars* fans read, talked on cell phones, or worked on laptop computers.

They drank from Pepsi cans that sported *Star Wars* characters. As the final hours approached, fans discarded their tents and chairs and stood in long lines. When the first ticket was sold at theaters from New York to Missouri to California, roars went up from the crowds that resounded across the nation.

On the other side of the Atlantic Ocean, British fans were packing their bags for a trip to the United States to see *The Phantom Menace*. For the first time, a movie opening had become a tourist event.

The first show at one minute after midnight on Wednesday, May 19th, played on 2,970 screens. The film's opening day set a new record by taking in $28,542,349. Within five days the film had grossed over $100 million. By the 13th day, it had crossed the $200 million line.

And Ewan McGregor had become an international star.

A fan clowns around with his light saber while waiting in line for tickets to Star Wars: Episode I—The Phantom Menace. *Die-hard fans camped outside of movie theaters for days to get tickets for the eagerly awaited prequel.*

2

SCHOOL DAZE

Ewan Gordon McGregor was born on March 31, 1971, in Perth, Scotland, and grew up in nearby Crieff, a town of around 6,000. Here the plains of the Lowlands changed dramatically into the wilder Highlands with its hills and mountains. As a child, Ewan enjoyed the outdoors and the vast greenness that surrounded him.

His acting career began at age six in a Sunday School play, *David and Goliath*. Ewan played the role of David. He couldn't read the lines in the play, but his mom, Carol, helped him memorize them. His minister remembered Ewan's debut performance as quite good.

A few weeks later, his parents, who were both teachers, took an excited Ewan and his older brother, Colin, to see his uncle in a new movie called *Star Wars*. Ewan was in awe of his mother's brother. Denis Lawson had grown up in Crieff, too, but had left the town to make his living as an actor. When he returned to Crieff for visits, his appearance raised many eyebrows.

"I remember throughout my childhood in the seventies, he used to come up and see us and he'd always look really

---

A Scottish bagpiper, wearing a traditional plaid kilt. Ewan McGregor grew up in the Scottish Lowlands. Nearby hills and woods were part of his childhood, and he always enjoyed the green and beautiful countryside.

A scene from the original Star Wars. *Ewan's uncle played a rogue commander in a few crucial scenes. This fascinated young Ewan, who wondered how actors could convincingly play characters so different from themselves.*

different from other people I knew," Ewan recalled. "He had flares on and sideburns and beads and a big sheepskin waistcoat and didn't wear any shoes, and I just wanted to be like him."

Denis Lawson didn't have a large part in *Star Wars*, but six-year-old Ewan was mesmerized when he watched his uncle command the Rogue X-Wing Squadron. Ewan was transported to the far-off galaxy. He wondered how his uncle could convincingly become someone else besides himself.

Ewan started watching old movies. On weekends he'd watch several black-and-white movies from the 1940s and 1950s. He was simply entranced by the world each movie created.

By the time he was nine, he'd decided to become an actor. Nothing else would do. But how did a nine-year-old prepare for an acting career? Ewan didn't have a clue, but he knew it would happen.

In his own way, Ewan taught himself how to act by mimicking his heroes. He taped a poster of Elvis Presley on his bedroom wall and imitated the strut and swagger he saw in Elvis's movies. Later the film *Grease* captured his attention, and he pretended he was the lead actor, singing and dancing even on the playground at school.

Young Ewan attended prestigious Morrison's Academy. His grandfather, three aunts, two uncles, father, mother, and brother had gone to school there. Since Ewan's father, Jim, taught physical education at Morrison's, Ewan could attend tuition-free, earn a first-rate education, and make contacts at the exclusive school.

But academics didn't appeal to Ewan. He was quite the opposite of his brother, who flew through the courses and was named head boy, which is equivalent to an American high school valedictorian. Colin was also quite athletic and was named captain of the cricket team. Ewan preferred solitary sports like swimming or golf to team sports.

He loved horses and riding across the Lowlands at a gallop. Although he didn't own a horse, as a teenager he worked at a local stable and rode the horses there. Ewan soon became an expert rider.

Music was also his passion. Ewan played the French horn in the school orchestra, sang in the choir, and volunteered for solos whenever possible. But his musical tastes were changing.

Down came the poster of Elvis, and up went one of Billy Idol. Ewan now played drums for Scarlet Pride, a rock band. He covered his spiked hair with red paint and wore bandannas around his knees when he beat out a rhythm on the drums.

Always a mischievous boy, as a teenager Ewan became a troublemaker. He wasn't in any serious trouble, but he would throw cones from the fir trees at girls or light fireworks and watch them skitter toward unsuspecting people walking on the road. He was thrown off a golf course for swearing at the top of his lungs after every bad shot. He took up smoking and drinking with friends. Weekends were a party, and the dreaded Monday morning and school came all too soon to suit Ewan.

"I wasn't interested in school. I got into trouble all the time and they kept saying: Attitude problem. I was unaware I had one because I had one, and it was starting to embarrass my father."

He still wanted to be an actor, but he made few attempts to work toward that goal. His disinterest in school included the drama department, and he didn't try out for parts in school plays. He sank further and further into what his parents saw as a depressed state.

His parents talked with him. The rector at the church spoke with him. But no one could convince Ewan that he needed an education to fall back on if he didn't make it as an actor. Finally, his parents gave in.

On a stormy night, Ewan's mother told him that she and his father had made the decision. Although it was hard for them as educators to accept, she told him that he could drop out of school and pursue his dream of being an actor.

Ewan quickly landed a job as a stagehand at the Perth Repertory Theatre. He shifted

Ewan jokes with photographers, looking very much like the goofy teenager he once was. As a youth Ewan became a prankster and eventually dropped out of school. But working in a local theater gave him new direction and sealed his decision to become an actor.

scenery, cleaned floors, and sold tickets—whatever had to be done.

"Suddenly I was where I wanted to be and my life went into wide-screen," Ewan said. "I had a ball and the depression lifted. But I was also a real pain in the backside because I was so keen. The people there remember me as a nightmare. I wanted to do everything—this, this, this, and this—and they would tell me to shut up." His curiosity and desire to learn never really offended the others at the theater because of his outgoing, friendly personality.

Soon he was onstage, but only as an extra. For his first professional acting job, he was listed in the program under "servants and others." He wore a black turban for the October 1987 production of *A Passage to India*. He admitted that he didn't actually act on stage, but just being there was enough to excite him and make him want to learn the craft.

He spoke to his parents about going to drama school. His enthusiasm was infectious, and they agreed that would be a good step—expensive, but a positive step forward.

Although he was only 17, Ewan packed his bags and left home when he was accepted at a one-year drama program in Kirkcaldy, a town of some 50,000. He studied the basics, from memorizing lines to learning where to stand on stage. He drew on an instinctive power within himself to become characters in plays. And he loved it. As inattentive as he had been at Morrison's Academy, he was the opposite at drama school.

His teachers realized that Ewan had a special talent and that he needed it stretched beyond the means of the one-year program at Kirkcaldy. A three-year program was suggested, but where should he go? His first choice was the Royal Academy of Dramatic Art in London. He prepared his audition, but only one man interviewed him. Once the man learned that Ewan was only 17, he dismissed him as too young and said he had years of auditions ahead of him.

It irritated Ewan that he wasn't even given a chance, but he continued his search for a new drama school. Uncle Denis Lawson helped him prepare for his audition at Guildhall School of Music and Drama, also in London. All prospective students were required to prepare three pieces: one from Shakespeare, one comic, and one of the student's choosing. Ewan worked very hard on his pieces, and his efforts were rewarded. He was one of 24 students accepted out of the 700 who had applied for the 1989 school year.

The course work was intense. Ewan's physical abilities were challenged through dance, mime, and acrobatics. He altered his voice for phonetics, dialects, and singing. And there were academic subjects as well. He studied theater history and text reading.

Ewan loved acting and he was good at it. One evening he was on stage in a wheelchair, performing a monologue that he'd written about an oil worker who'd lost one of his legs in an accident. His bit was going well until he forgot his lines. Instead of stepping out of character, he looked down at his stump of a leg and rubbed it until he remembered his lines. He thought his long pause had blown the performance, but discovered that wasn't true.

Sitting in the audience was a talent scout from Channel 4 of the British Broadcasting Company. After the show, he spoke with Ewan and asked if he would audition for a six-part miniseries for television. The only hitch was that the production was already in casting, and filming would start immediately after that. Ewan couldn't possibly stay in school and take the part. But that would be a moot point if he didn't get the part, so Ewan scheduled an audition.

He was offered the role. Ewan now faced a decision. It was March 1992 and he was mere months from graduating. Should he stay in school? If the point of this education was to get professional acting jobs, and here was one being offered, wouldn't he be crazy not to take it?

Ewan signed the contract.

3

STARTING OUT

E wan's first television role was in the six-part miniseries *Lipstick on Your Collar*, written by Dennis Potter. Besides scripts, the screenwriter had also penned nonfiction, fiction, and plays. Ewan felt honored to be cast in the legendary writer's production and spent time on and off the set with Potter.

"I'll never forget it," Ewan said. "We were doing a scene in a graveyard, and he came and sat down with me. I'd just had my 21st birthday on the set, and he said, 'When this comes out, you'll be offered loads of stuff, and you mustn't take the first thing that comes along. Take the things that come from your gut.'"

In *Lipstick on Your Collar*, Ewan played Mick Hopper, a private who worked for the military intelligence bureau in London during the Suez Canal Crisis of 1956. Hopper was the main character's best friend, and although Ewan did not have the lead role in the series, he played a part that echoed some of his own past. Hopper was a dreamer and an aspiring drummer. At times he'd break into song, jump on a table, and lip-synch to an Elvis Presley song. Ewan's

---

Tower Bridge in London, England. While just starting out as an actor, Ewan landed a role in a six-part miniseries and moved to London for filming. However, after the miniseries finished, Ewan went back to countless auditions before he won his next role.

practice of imitating Elvis back in his bedroom in Crieff came in handy on the set.

"I thought that when the first episode of *Lipstick* was aired my life would change dramatically," Ewan said. "I remember counting the days to the first transmission. But when it was screened nothing happened. Nobody recognized me. I didn't get mobbed. It was a huge anticlimax."

The offers for more jobs didn't pour in as Potter had predicted. Instead, Ewan spent four months going from audition to audition until he was hired for a very small part in the movie *Being Human*, starring Robin Williams.

Ewan traveled to Morocco in northern Africa in the fall of 1992 to play the part of Alvarez. His lines in the movie were, "I'll do it," and "That was a joke, that was a joke." Most of his time was spent having fun, but he also learned from watching the other actors. When he returned to London, it was for a brief stint in a play, *What the Butler Saw*. A few months later he packed his bags for a location shoot in France for a TV mini-series.

Ewan's next acting job was in *Scarlet and Black*, a remake of a 1954 film that was to be shown in three parts on television. In Britain actors moved back and forth from television to movies to television. One medium isn't viewed as superior to the other, as it is by many people in the United States.

Scarlet and Black was a period piece, set in the early 1800s. Ewan starred as Julien Sorel, a young man who still idolized Napoleon, even though the French leader had been defeated at Waterloo. Julien wanted to make something of himself and yearned to wear the scarlet tunic of a soldier, but instead was forced to wear the black robes of a priest.

As with all of his other acting jobs, Ewan learned more about his chosen profession with on-the-job training as he followed the director's orders and observed other actors. With *Scarlet and Black* on tape by mid-1993, Ewan returned to London and took a small part in a televised play, *Doggin' Around*.

Always auditioning for future work, Ewan read for a role in *Shallow Grave* for a new team of moviemakers. He was chosen to play Alex Law over several hundred other actors. This role was actually created for a Scot. Using his native accent was unusual for Ewan, who had learned a passable English accent for his other roles.

Shallow Grave was the first undertaking for Figment Films. The screenplay was written by John Hodge, who was a doctor. His sister had introduced him to her boss, up-and-coming filmmaker Andrew McDonald, who was thinking of producing his first feature film. The two hit it off immediately. They talked over the idea for *Shallow Grave* and worked together on the final version. With a completed script, McDonald lined up the money for the film, and the duo looked around for a good director. They didn't have a large budget, so they set their sights on someone who had talent, knew more than they did about the business, and wasn't terribly expensive. When they met director Danny Boyle, they knew he was a kindred spirit, and the trio formed Figment Films. Although not a part of the moviemaking team, Ewan also developed a close relationship with these men.

Shallow Grave is the story of three people who share a flat, which is what the British call an apartment. Ewan's character is a journalist. The other roommates are an overworked female doctor and an accountant. All three are very, very rude yuppies. The movie begins with them interviewing prospective flatmates for the fourth bedroom. They delight in making the interviewees squirm in discomfort. Finally they decide on a man and let him move in. When the man doesn't come out of his room for a couple days, they check on him and discover that he is dead. Under his bed they find a suitcase full of money.

Ewan's character wants to keep the money and dispose of the body. He convinces the others to go along with him and hatches a plan to bury the man in the woods. First, though, they must cut off his hands and feet and knock out his teeth so that he can't be identified. No one wants to do that, so they draw straws for the job. The accountant draws the short straw and must do the dirty work, which drives him quite mad.

The movie is a black comedy with a British twist. More murders, a cover-up, and friends turning on friends complicate the plot. At the end of the film, Ewan's character is pinned to the floor with a butcher knife through his chest.

To prepare for the part of the arrogant Alex, an aggressive, obnoxious person, Ewan listened to tapes of comedians belittling people. He spent time in the newsroom of the *Evening Times*, the newspaper in Glasgow, Scotland, learning how a journalist would react to life. He wanted to be a convincing partner in crime.

Director Danny Boyle decided that he, the three main actors, and his partners MacDonald and Hodge should live together in a flat during the rehearsal period. Since the film was based on three people knowing each other very well, the experience of living together jelled the cast.

"The rehearsal period was brilliant from the

Ewan (right), Keith Allen (left), and Kerry Fox in the movie Shallow Grave. *The film was a huge success in Britain when it opened in 1994. It also made a big name for Ewan throughout Europe.*

word go," Ewan said. "We used to get up, have breakfast, and do scenes in our pajamas."

By avoiding the London movie district, the production company lowered costs. The main set of the film was a large four-bedroom flat, which was built inside a huge warehouse in a Glasgow industrial complex. Exterior scenes were shot in central Scotland.

When shooting ended, Ewan made a few guest shots on television series. While filming an episode of the popular courtroom drama *Kavanagh QC*, he met Eve Mavrakis. Eve (pronounced Ev) was a production designer from France, seven years older than Ewan. After their first hello, Ewan knew this woman would become a major part of his life.

During October and November of 1994, Ewan traveled to the coast of Cornwall, in southwest

Ewan and fellow actor Yoshi Oida in a scene from the 1996 film The Pillow Book. *During filming, Ewan became quite an international traveler, flying to Luxembourg, Japan, and Hong Kong.*

England, to film another movie. In *Blue Juice* Ewan was cast as Dean Raymond, a drug dealer and aspiring tabloid journalist, who was part of a surfing group that hung around the coast during the summer. Ewan thought the film was a bit muddled in the middle and just not very good overall, but it was work.

Next he traveled to Luxembourg to shoot *The Pillow Book*, written and directed by controversial independent filmmaker Peter Greenaway, whose work Ewan admired. Some location shooting was done in Japan and Hong Kong, so Ewan was becoming quite an international traveler.

In *The Pillow Book*, Ewan played the very unusual role of Jerome in quite a unique story. A Japanese woman wrote chapters of her book on Jerome's nude body. Then he would go to the publisher where clerks would copy the words from his skin.

Ewan's makeup call took hours. He'd arrive at the studio around four in the morning and lie on his back for a couple of hours while his front was painted. Usually he fell asleep. For the next two hours, he stood up while an artist wrote on his backside.

Regarding himself as something of a free spirit, Ewan didn't mind being nude in the art film because it was an integral part of the story. "It's ultimately more embarrassing for everyone on the set," he said. "They're all trying desperately not to look." He said that he didn't really feel nude with the words written on him. They gave him the feeling of wearing clothes.

By the time he finished filming *The Pillow Book* in early 1995, Ewan had acted in four motion pictures and several TV shows. He'd received some attention from the public when his television mini-series and guest spots had aired. But it was nothing compared to the acclaim he received when *Shallow Grave* hit the theaters. His star was starting to climb.

4

THE
BIG BREAK

W hen *Shallow Grave* opened in Britain, people waited in long lines to see the movie. It became the biggest British moneymaker of the year and won film awards in France, Spain, Portugal, Italy, and in America at Robert Redford's Sundance Film Festival.

For many people in Europe the film restored their faith in British movies. But reviews were mixed when the film opened in the United States. It was the blackest of black comedies with particular British humor, which didn't play well with American audiences. Several reviewers commented on the fine quality of acting but didn't single out Ewan. However, his became a big name in Europe.

And his name was very important to that trio of filmmakers, Boyle, McDonald, and Hodge. With two stipulations, they had already cast Ewan in their next film. He would have to lose 28 pounds and shave his head. While he was filming *The Pillow Book*, Ewan was already losing weight, and scenes shot at the end of that production showed him considerably thinner than those shot at the beginning.

Ewan's other big break came in the 1996 movie Trainspotting. *Although Ewan had never used heroin, he wanted to be able to portray an addict in a realistic way. Before filming began he read books on crack and heroin and worked with recovering heroin addicts in Scotland.*

The weight loss was necessary for Ewan's role as Mark Renton, an emaciated heroin addict in *Trainspotting*. Hodge's script was based on the oddly titled 1993 book by Irvine Welsh. The author explained the title as "the compulsive collecting of locomotive engine numbers from the British railway system. But you can't do anything with the numbers once you've collected them." Hodge called it a metaphor "for doing something that gives your life a bit of structure but is ultimately point-less." Ewan's take on the title was that "heroin users mainline along their arms and inject up and down on the main vein. 'Station to station,' they call it. And for addicts, everything narrows down to that one goal of getting drugs. Maybe 'trainspotters' are like that, obsessively taking down the numbers of trains."

The book reads like a collection of short stories from several different characters' view-points with lots of internal dialogue. Hodge argued that it couldn't be made into a movie, but his partners convinced him otherwise. He wrote the script with Renton as the main char-acter interacting with his friends, lowlifes, and junkies in Edinburgh, Scotland.

To prepare for the role Ewan said, "I read books on crack and heroin. Then I went up to Glasgow and met people from the Calton Athletic Recovery Group, which is an organi-zation of recovering heroin addicts who don't use methadone to come off [the drug]; they just come off day by day."

Ewan and the other actors in the movie developed a working relationship with the for-mer addicts. "I've never shot drugs," Ewan said. "But we did 'cookery' classes at Calton. It was six actors sitting around a table with little bits of glucose powder." They wanted the movie to be realistic and scenes to appear as if the characters were melting heroin. "Listening to these guys' experiences, the point of despair most of them had reached was extraordinary."

Trainspotting was shot in seven weeks in the summer of 1995, first in Glasgow and then in London. No scene was over two minutes long, and the camera angles were all over the place, high and low. The film showed the highs of heroin and the lows of drug addiction. It contained violence, death, sex, fantasy, and hallucinations, but basically was a story of the friendship and betrayal of addicts.

The shoestring budget of $2.5 million was kept low by using no special effects. When Ewan's character was to sink into the floor during a heroin overdose, he lay atop a platform over a trap door and was lowered down. When a dog was to jump up and down as if it had been shot, the director screamed at it until the dog jumped. "Because we had no money for this film," Ewan said, "all these effects are really thrown together, with absolutely no technology whatever."

In July, shortly after filming was over, Ewan and Eve borrowed a French villa for a week-long party. The culmination of the festivities was their exchange of wedding vows. Sixty friends and family members witnessed the ceremony. The local mayor conducted the wedding in French. Ewan only knew a few words in the foreign language, but said, "Oui," when prompted. He didn't know what was said, but he understood the meaning of the ceremony, and he knew he loved Eve and wanted to spend the rest of his life with her.

The happy couple barely had time to recover

from the party when they returned to England for Ewan to start work on another film, an adaptation of Jane Austen's *Emma*. Ewan's normally busy life seemed busier than ever as he jumped from movie to movie.

"On the first day of shooting, I was riding horses and wearing a top hat, tails, and gloves. And I realized that three weeks before, I'd been lying on a floor in Scotland with a skinned head and needles and syringes all around. I wondered what I was doing. Yet I enjoyed it." Ewan has described himself as a workaholic and likes to know what his next project is long before his current one is over.

"I really like being an actor," Ewan has said, "which means that the most exciting part about it for me is that you get to learn about so many different things—and that you get to play all sorts of different people. I would get terribly bored if I was playing the same kind of character all the time."

In the romantic comedy *Emma*, Ewan's role was the aristocrat Frank Churchill, a debonair English scoundrel. Churchill was the love interest of the main character, played by Gwyneth Paltrow. "I play a kind of frightfully charming character," Ewan said. "I think everyone will hate him."

For this aristocratic role, Ewan practiced a clipped English accent that would fit the suave character. Yet when he wasn't in front of the camera, he spent hours in his trailer listening to tapes of Yorkshire accents and memorizing lines for his next movie.

When filming wrapped up on *Emma*, Ewan rushed straight from that set to the former mining village of Grimethorpe in Yorkshire,

Ewan with Polly Walker in Emma. *His character, Frank Churchill, was a 19th century English scoundrel, which was quite a change from the role he had just finished in* Trainspotting.

In the movie Brassed Off, *Ewan (here left, with Tara Fitzgerald, center, and Pete Postlethwaite, right) portrayed Andy, a young miner who plays in a community brass band. Since Ewan had played the French horn as a boy, he was a natural in the film's musical scenes.*

England. Others in the cast for *Brassed Off* had arrived on the set a week earlier.

What a change to go from period costumes to more contemporary clothes again! Just as *Emma* had reflected society as it was in 19th-century England, *Brassed Off* reflected the 1992 political situation in England. Many coal mines, called collieries, were being closed by the government to make way for nuclear power. When a colliery closed, it put most of the town out of work, creating near-ghost towns.

Brassed Off, which means "ticked off" in American slang, has a double meaning in the movie. Many institutions in England, such as schools, factories, and collieries, have their own brass bands. In the fictional town of Grimley, which was based on Grimethorpe, the colliery's band had been a proud tradition for a hundred years. At the time the movie takes place the government is pushing to close the colliery.

Ewan's role was Andy, a young miner who played a tenor horn in the brass band. Since Ewan had played the French horn when he was in school, he had no trouble with the musical part. Joining the all-male band was Gloria, who recently returned to the village. When they were teens, Gloria and Andy were romantically involved. They again are attracted to each other, and their relationship evolves until the band discovers Gloria is working for the government.

When the mine is closed, and the band leader is in the hospital with black lung disease, the band decides to call it quits. But since they qualified to represent the town in a national competition, they regroup (with a check from Gloria for expenses) and take off for the big contest. In a powerful ending, the band wins first place. Even though the town is suffering the hardships of the mine closing, they are filled with pride for their band.

Ewan liked the film and the human rights message behind it, although he claimed he isn't politically oriented. "Party politics bore me. I'm political in that I'm incredibly aware and passionate about how people are treated."

He also liked working with independent film-makers and was proud of his roles, but he wanted to ensure that he'd be in character-driven films. With six of his friends, he formed a production company named Natural Nylon. "Natural" was the group's attitude and "Nylon" was a combination of New York and London, representing the international world where their innovative films would debut. They hoped to have more input and maintain more control over their work by choosing the films and casting one or more of their members in each film. They tossed out ideas for future projects and began exploring each one.

Besides looking forward to his new business venture, Ewan was also looking forward to the release of four movies in 1996. He'd played incredibly different characters, and he wondered how the public would react to his work. The first film to come out was *Trainspotting.* Reception was mixed, but the film was quite a financial success.

Some critics thought the movie glamorized heroin. Ewan defended the movie. "*Trainspotting* doesn't make the heroin look slick. The reason people get upset about it is because they don't want to think about drugs as being the least bit pleasurable, but heroin makes you feel great—apparently—and we showed the people who do it feeling great in the movie. But then we show what happens if you get addicted, what happens to you as you die."

He argued that the firm presented an even-handed picture of drug addiction. "If someone's constantly telling you 'Don't do this, don't do that,' especially as a kid—the first thing you want to do is go and do it. It's much more responsible to say 'It'll make you feel fantastic for a short while but then it will lead to this, this, and this.'"

The reception to Ewan's role in the film was outstanding and netted him several acting awards in Britain. Much of the film's success rested on his charismatic performance, which made audiences care about a heroin addict. But he didn't dwell on the praise he was receiving. His professional life was about to be eclipsed by his private life.

5

FILM
AFTER FILM

In February 1996, Ewan rushed Eve to the hospital to give birth to their daughter. He was unprepared for the huge event. "I imagined you had to be this rock for your wife and I just got more and more frightened the longer it went on, that something was going to go wrong. In the end she had a Cesarean section and I had to go in there and all I was thinking was 'Oh no, I'm not big enough for this, not quite sure if I can handle this one.'"

The actor, who could take on any role and make it his own, was apprehensive about his role as a parent. But he managed, Eve survived, and they welcomed Clara Mathilde McGregor into their lives.

Ewan was reluctant to leave his wife and newborn baby, but a prior contract required him to film *Nightwatch* in the United States. "I went to L.A. to make *Nightwatch* because I wanted to have the kind of exposure that would allow me to pick and choose my films. You can't do that if you just make little independent British films."

He was amazed at the British press for making a big

Ewan in a scene from Nightwatch. *His character is a security guard at a city morgue who is unjustly suspected of serial murders. Although Ewan went to Los Angeles to make the film, he made it clear that he had no intention of moving to America. He just wants to go "wherever the good scripts come from."*

deal of his going to America. After all, he had also made films in France, Japan, Hong Kong, Africa, and Luxembourg. He had no intention of living in the United States as some British actors do. "At the moment there is good stuff coming out of Britain. I will just go where the work is. Wherever the good scripts come from."

He appeared outraged when interviewers asked if he was selling out to Hollywood. "What I am is an actor, and stardom isn't important to me. Success is what I strive for, not stardom. I just want to be as good as I can."

In *Nightwatch*, Ewan played the role of Martin Bells, a law student who works nights as a security guard at the city morgue. His character is unjustly suspected of serial murders. For this psychological thriller, Ewan worked on an American accent. Immediately after filming was finished, Ewan flew home. He missed his wife and baby and vowed to take them with him on future location shoots.

Life in London was hectic, and he loved it. He played golf when he could, and he rode his motorcycle as much as possible. However, his face was very well-known in Britain by that time, and privacy was a thing of the past. But he still hung out at pubs with friends, notably guys from the musical group Oasis. Ewan liked going out, and Eve liked staying home. He called their relationship a balance.

On the first day of July, when Ewan began filming *The Serpent's Kiss* in the Irish village of Sixmilebridge, his wife and baby were with him. He carried Clara around the movie set and played with her during lunch and dinner breaks. She was growing so quickly, and Ewan didn't want to miss any of her changes.

When Ewan had agreed to do *The Serpent's*

Kiss, it easily worked into his schedule. But filming was delayed nearly a year because of the search for just the right house as a setting for the historical film. By then Ewan had been offered other movies, but he declined them and honored his agreement to film *The Serpent's Kiss*. "If you're going to commit to do something, you should do it," he said, reaffirming his philosophy of life. "It's dangerous territory when you start agreeing to do lots of jobs and then taking only the ones which will give you the most money. That's not going to do you any good in the long run."

Producer Robert Jones was pleased that Ewan kept his word. "Ewan is a joy to work with. He's incredibly focused and a very genuine guy. . . . Everybody wants to work with him."

The Serpent's Kiss is set in England in 1699. Ewan wore a long curly wig and gentlemen's breeches for his role as Dutch landscape gardener Meneer Chrome, who is hired to transform the grounds of an estate into an extravagant garden. The tale is like a soap opera, with Ewan's character seducing both the landlord's wife and daughter and being blackmailed by the wife's cousin.

Ewan spent quiet evenings with his wife and daughter instead of his usual carousing with other actors at local pubs. Members of the crew had high praise for him as a person. His father summed up the feelings on the set. "His mum and I have been on the set of most of his films and the comment we always get is how nice he is. It doesn't matter if you're the guy who makes the tea or the director, Ewan chats and makes friends with everybody."

Ewan's folks are among his biggest fans,

and Ewan respects and admires them for letting him quit regular school, attend drama school, and follow his dream. Knowing his parents' routine of taking friends to see his movies when they are released, he felt a bit apprehensive before the summer release of *The Pillow Book.* He warned his parents about the nude scenes and the story content. After they saw the movie, they faxed him that they thought the artsy movie, which at times had several frames on the screen at once, was beautiful.

In Fall 1996, Ewan's busy schedule took him to Utah for the filming of the new Boyle-McDonald-Hodge movie, *A Life Less Ordinary.* Ewan was excited to be working with the threesome again. He was allowed to create a scene and decide, along with the director, how to shoot it. It made him feel satisfied as an actor.

Producer McDonald admired Ewan's work. "He looks ordinary, but he's magic-looking on camera. No questions, he's part of our core team. It's four of us now."

In *A Life Less Ordinary*, Ewan played Robert, a Scottish immigrant in America. In one day Robert loses his girlfriend, his job as a janitor, and his apartment. In desperation, he kidnaps Celine, the daughter of his wealthy former employer. Robert is a bumbling abductor, and Celine takes over as negotiator. The plot is complicated by two angels sent to make sure Robert and Celine fall in love.

Cameron Diaz starred as Celine. She and Ewan hit it off immediately; both are warm and friendly without movie-star attitudes. Diaz praised her costar. "He makes acting seem so easy. . . . He's charming and funny and, you know, all those things that all the girls want. He's just got it."

Eve and Clara lived with Ewan in a rental house for the three-month shoot. Eve worked as a production designer on the film. On breaks in the filming Ewan stepped out of his character's persona and became a father, playing with and singing to Clara.

On weekends Ewan partied with the crew at a biker bar, and he said that everyone had a great time filming in picturesque Utah. The local citizens "made us feel so welcome there on the whole. We had a really nice time there, and it's a beautiful, beautiful state," he later

In A Life Less Ordinary, Ewan played a bumbling kidnapper. He and his costar, Cameron Diaz, found each other to be charming and down-to-earth, without any movie star attitudes.

*Julianna Margulies (left) and Ewan in a scene from the television series ER.
Ewan was nominated for an Emmy Award for his guest appearance, in which he
played a robber who takes hostages after trying to hold up a convenience store.*

recalled. Ewan's straightforward streak made him add, "However, Salt Lake City is a rather strange town."

While in the U.S., Ewan was contracted for a guest appearance on his favorite TV show, *ER*. He played Duncan, a Scotsman who robs a convenience store with his American cousin. The robbery goes awry and Duncan takes hostages, including Carol, one of *ER*'s nurses, played by Julianna Margulies. In the end he is shot and dies on the operating table.

Ewan admitted being starstruck as he worked with actors he'd watched each week on television. The episode was one of the highlights of Ewan's visit to the United States.

But there were many more highlights waiting around the corner.

6

NEW AND
DIFFERENT ROLES

When Ewan and his family returned to England from the United States after filming *A Life Less Ordinary*, he took some time off from making back-to-back films. He bought a house for his family. While the house was being remodeled, he wanted to spend quality time with Eve and Clara. The holiday atmosphere quickly changed to one of anxiety when Clara was diagnosed with meningitis, a disease that attacks membranes around the brain and spinal cord. Sick with worry, Ewan snapped angrily at a reporter who turned up on his doorstep asking questions about his daughter. Fortunately, Clara made a full recovery from the disease.

Although Ewan takes his family on location shoots so he doesn't separate his family life from his professional life as an actor, he does separate his private life from his public life. Fiercely protective of Clara and Eve, Ewan rarely poses for publicity pictures with his family and has released pictures of the family to the press instead.

Ewan is a devoted father, but he admitted he'd neglected

Ewan and his wife, Eve. Although Ewan brings his family on locations, he keeps his private life very separate from his public life. He rarely allows Eve or their daughter, Clara, to be photographed by the press.

one part of his daughter's world. Since Eve's first language is French, Clara's first words were in that language too. The little girl said "Au revoir" instead of "Goodbye." Ewan decided he'd better learn more French, or as his daughter grew older she'd argue with him in words he couldn't understand.

In February 1997 Ewan returned to his roots in Crieff, Scotland. Morrison's Academy welcomed him not as a returning dropout but as a movie star. He spoke to a student assembly of fifth- and sixth-year students about the British film industry. When interviewed for the yearbook, he was asked if he regretted dropping out of Guildhall School of Music and Drama when he was so close to finishing. "I don't regret it at all, no. What I do regret, however, is not having realized that what you are taught in school is maybe valid. I never really made the connection that what you were being taught was useful in any way. I never thought it was and I was wrong in that respect." Later that day, Ewan met with the cast of the school production of *Tom Sawyer* and showed them what he'd learned since he'd left the school. He worked with the cast on the choreography of the graveyard fight scene.

In early March 1997, Ewan's short break from moviemaking was over, and he reported to the set of *Velvet Goldmine*, a gay love story set amid the 1970s and 1980s glitter rock scene in London. In America this movement later developed into the punk and heavy metal sounds. "I play an American rock 'n' roll star who comes to work in England and meets a sticky end," Ewan said. "I wear lots of long bleached blond wigs, leather trousers, and hipster flares. I'm quite grungy. It's the other actors who look high camp. My character isn't based on anyone

In the film Velvet Goldmine, *Ewan's teenaged dream of being a rock star came true. He liked the independent film's depiction of the glitter rock era, and he even got to sing in the concert scenes.*

in particular, but I did watch Iggy Pop videos to get his incredible moves down."

Back in his school days, Ewan had played in the band Scarlet Pride. Now he brought his teen fantasy of being a rock star a few steps closer and understood the difference between being a musician and an actor. "It's the idea of standing there in front of all those thousands of people. It's just you, it's your music, it's not about pretending to be someone else. I don't have the guts but I would love to know what that feels like."

Although Ewan admitted feeling uncomfortable with the gay love scenes in *Velvet Goldmine*, he liked the portrayal of the outlandish rock era in the independent film, and he liked singing in the concert scenes. A bonus was that the set was only a short drive from his home. He could go to work and then return home like a regular guy. Eve and Clara didn't have to be uprooted and whisked to some far-away location.

For three months Ewan worked on *Velvet Goldmine.* When that shoot wrapped, he turned his attention to *Star Wars: Episode I—The Phantom Menace.* Ewan's character, Obi-Wan Kenobi, was an old man, played by Sir Alec Guinness, in the original *Star Wars* trilogy. Ewan wanted his portrayal of the younger Obi-Wan to lead naturally to the older character. "I have to get his accent. He's got this very specific older man's voice. It'd be great if I could trace it back to his youth and get it right." He watched and studied old Alec Guinness films to hear the inflection of the man's voice when he was much younger.

What would Obi-Wan be without his light saber? Ewan was offered his choice of weapon, but as with other aspects of the movie, its shape and color were secret. "This guy looked me in the eye and said, 'Are you ready?' Then he opened up a briefcase-sized box with eight or nine light-saber handles. I picked the sexiest one. I realized, I've been waiting 20 years to have my own light saber."

Major filming was done at the sprawling Leavesden Studios, just outside of London. The 300-acre film center was completely surrounded by barbed wire, policed by guard dogs, and required picture IDs and computerized cards for entrance at the checkpoint. Strict secrecy demanded that few people saw the entire script. Many actors only saw the pages where their characters appeared.

More than 57 sets were built at the studio, but most of Ewan's acting was in front of blue screens. After each day's 12-hour shoot, the film was digitally transmitted to Los Angeles to Industrial Light & Magic, creator George Lucas's special effects company. Computer-generated images were added and sent back by morning for Lucas to view. The eight-hour difference in London and Los Angeles time zones allowed the work to progress in this timely fashion. There were a total of 2,200 special-effects shots in *The Phantom Menace*.

"The work was so complex with all the special effects and stuff that I found myself hanging around for days. What bothered me most was that everything was so deliberate," Ewan said. Director George Lucas told him exactly where to stand so that a background could be added digitally later.

"There was no spontaneity. Your job, as an actor, was just to get it out. I was frowning a lot. It just became a frowning exercise."

In July the cast and crew moved to Italy to film at the Royal Palace. Later that month they moved to a 15-square-mile desert land in Tunisia. Actors, including Ewan, arrived on the set by sunrise so that most of the filming was concluded before the heat of the day, which reached over 130 degrees in the shade. For this 10-day shoot, Ewan left his family in London. He yearned for the "dreary weather of good ol' London and the gentle tapping of rain against the windowpanes while watching Clara sleep in her bed." When the desert scenes were finished, the actors returned to London for final filming.

In this scene from Star Wars: Episode I—The Phantom Menace, *Obi-Wan Kenobi (Ewan, right) and Qui-Gon Jinn (Liam Neeson, left) battle the evil Darth Maul (Ray Stark, center). Many of Ewan's scenes were actually filmed in front of blue screens so that computerized special effects could be added later.*

The first episode is set 40 years before the fourth episode, the original *Star Wars*. The story follows a young Anakin Skywalker, who later matures into the Jedi from the dark side, Darth Vader, father of Luke and Leia. Jedi master Qui-Gon Jinn, protector of the Old Republic, sees something special, perhaps The Force, in the boy. The Jedi council disagrees. Yoda, its leader, senses great fear in Anakin: "Fear is the path to the dark side. Fear leads to anger; anger leads to hate; hate leads to suffering." In his death scene,

Qui-Gon asks his apprentice Obi-Wan Kenobi, Ewan's character, to train Anakin to be a Jedi. Obi-Wan agrees.

Ewan's role will be featured in the second (release date of 2002) and third (estimated release date of 2005) episodes. In June 2000, Ewan will report to Australia to begin filming the second episode. But the workaholic certainly couldn't remain idle between *Star Wars* movies.

WHAT LIES AHEAD?

By the end of September 1997, principal photography on *The Phantom Menace* was completed. In October, Ewan's busy schedule took him to Scarborough in northeast England for the location filming of *Little Voice*. Although his part was small, it was pivotal. He played Billy, a telephone repairman with a passion for homing pigeons. He develops a crush on Little Voice, a shy woman who can mimic the voices of stars Judy Garland, Billie Holiday, and Marilyn Monroe. Little Voice falls into the hands of an aggressive agent, and Billy helps her break free.

Although the cast did not complete filming until late December 1997, Ewan wrapped up his part near midnight on Sunday, November 16. Nine hours later he was on the set of his next movie, *Rogue Trader*, in a London studio.

Rogue Trader is based on Nick Leeson's autobiography. Ewan played Leeson, a futures broker based in Singapore, who brought down London's Barings Bank. Most of the shooting was done in London with mainly exterior shots filmed in Malaysia, Indonesia, and Singapore.

Ewan made the foreign trips on his own, since they

Ewan is a multitalented actor. The movie Rogue Trader *gave him an opportunity to play a different kind of role—a futures broker based in Singapore, who brought down London's Barings Bank. The filming of the movie also required him to travel to many Southeast Asian countries.*

were fairly quick hops, and returned to London at the end of January 1998. He rearranged his schedule to take the entire month of February off to relax with his family.

In early spring he was back at work on yet another film, his 15th in just five years. The American independent thriller *Eye of the Beholder* was filmed in Montreal, Canada. Ewan played a nameless private eye, who for 10 years followed a woman and discovered she was a serial killer.

When the film was completed, Ewan returned to London for the final reshoots for *The Phantom Menace* and then he took another block of time off again to be with his family.

For well over a year, Ewan had believed he would star in the Boyle-McDonald-Hodge movie *The Beach*. He felt betrayed when he learned that the British moviemaking trio had cast Leonardo DiCaprio in the role that Ewan had thought was his. Boyle explained to Ewan that the decision was all about money. The film-makers could get more financing from an American studio if they had a bigger star. Ewan had always been somewhat scornful of the Hollywood movie machine, and this solidi-fied his opinion and disillusioned him about his friends. "I guess that's the way business is supposed to work, but when we were all just mates, it was never about money but about making intelligent films. I think something got lost in the process."

For a change of pace, Ewan then signed on to star in the stage production *Little Malcolm and His Struggle Against the Eunuchs*. His uncle, Denis Lawson, directed the play at the 174-seat Hampstead Theatre Club in north London. "With the British love of building someone up and then tearing them down, I'm setting myself up for some serious abuse," Ewan said. "But I really miss the whole process of rehearsing with a bunch of people. And that paralyzing fear of the first night and the adrenaline rush that comes afterwards." The sold-out play earned positive reviews, and it opened for an eight-week run in January 1999 at London's Comedy Theatre.

The play was a joy for Ewan, but it wasn't long before he was off to Ireland for the filming of *Nora*, a project partially underwritten by his and his friends' company Natural Nylon. In this movie he played writer James Joyce. For this role Ewan researched minute details about the writer, who earned both high praise and ridicule for his literary works.

Next on Ewan's plate was *Moulin Rouge*, a movie about a young poet who defies his father and moves to Paris. Ewan's character falls for the star of a nightclub in a doomed love affair. Although not a fully scored musical, this film features some scenes with songs. Shooting is scheduled for October 1999 through February 2000 in Australia. Ewan will have a few months off before returning down under in June to shoot *Star Wars: Episode II*.

And then? Who knows? With the release of *The Phantom Menace*, Ewan McGregor is now a household name. Will that sort of fame change the uninhibited actor who normally speaks his mind and takes movie projects not for the money, but because he likes the script?

"I knew it was going to be enormous when it came out, and I've never been in anything like that before. I wondered how it would juxtapose with the other work I was doing. Some of the actors in the original *Star Wars* didn't do anything else afterwards, and I wondered, is that going to happen to me?"

Before he took the role, Ewan asked advice from his uncle, whose film career includes some wonderful movies, but who is known best by fans for his role as the fighter pilot in the earlier three episodes. Would Ewan's fine film work take a backseat to his holding a light saber? But the choice was easily made. "I mean," Ewan said, "when someone wanders up and says, 'Do you want to be in a new *Star Wars* movie?' it would take a bigger man than me to say no." Now he must live with that choice.

Director George Lucas is not very concerned. "Ewan's talent will win out over everything. He's got a great future. He will survive *Star Wars*."

Other directors have praised Ewan's talent as well. He may not have been well-known in America before the *Star Wars* adventure began, but in Europe he'd made a name for himself in independent films long before he was cast as Obi-Wan Kenobi. His well-earned reputation as a lovable rogue came through in his work. *Trainspotting* director Danny Boyle once said, "Every now and then you come across someone who's a sort of spokesperson for a particular era, someone who sums up a particular feeling or mood. Well, Ewan is one of those people. He is such a contrast to the kind of naked ambition and hardness of the '80s."

Mark Herman, who directed Ewan in *Brassed Off*, said, "Ewan's got the world at his feet and that makes this a dangerous time for him."

The British press have called Ewan a very grounded actor who hasn't forgotten his roots. He doesn't like self-promotion, especially on television. In his interviews with magazine reporters, he's slipped in a taboo word or two.

Britain's Prince Charles, left, greets Ewan at the royal premiere of Star Wars: Episode I—The Phantom Menace. *Meeting royalty is one of the results of Ewan's fame, but he remains a down-to-earth guy who still chooses his movie projects based on the quality of their scripts rather than the size of their budgets.*

He claims, "No one can swear like a Scotsman." But after his father reminded him that his foul language embarrassed people back home, Ewan has tried to watch his use of it.

He's still outspoken, but that quality may become toned down. Ewan already admits, "Whenever I do a press junket, I always get really depressed afterwards. . . . Frightened about what I've said. The idea of it—why is everybody so interested? Why am I the one? There are moments of real, sweaty terror in the middle of the night. Panicking. *Panicking.* Not being able to sleep because it's not natural to talk about yourself all day."

He concentrates on his film roles in interviews and rarely mentions a different side of his personality—the side that raises funds for Comic Relief charities or visits with kids at a children's hospice. He cares for people and sees the positive side of situations.

Ewan's twinkling eyes, his reckless grin, and his unself-conscious nature make him an attractive actor. He's been on several magazines' sexiest-man lists, and his following of fans ranges from screaming school girls to sedate men who see Ewan as a strong character actor.

His various roles have demanded that he look entirely different in each film. The heroin addict, the Jedi knight, the pigeon handler, the gay rock singer, the coal miner—all stretched the acting ability of Ewan McGregor. But he has skillfully handled every one of them.

What will the new century hold for the Scot? Will the unaffected, open, and natural Ewan change with fame? Probably not. His reputation as a bloke's bloke, as a man on the street, as a regular guy, will endure as his film career soars toward the stars in a galaxy far, far away.

CHRONOLOGY

1971	Born on March 31 to Carol and James McGregor in Perth, Scotland.
1977	Sees his uncle perform in *Star Wars*.
1980	Decides he wants to be an actor.
1987	Drops out of Morrison's Academy; makes professional acting debut at the Perth Repertory Theatre.
1988	Attends a drama school in Kirkcaldy, Scotland.
1989–92	Attends Guildhall School of Music and Drama in London.
1992	Lands first television miniseries role in *Lipstick on Your Collar*.
1993	Meets British filmmakers Danny Boyle, Andrew McDonald, and John Hodge; accepts lead role and begins working on their first movie, *Shallow Grave*.
1994	*Shallow Grave* is released; becomes a star in Britain and Europe.
1995	Marries Eve Mavrakis in France.
1996	Daughter, Clara Mathilde, is born; wins Best British Actor at *Empire Magazine* Awards.
1997	Wins Best Actor for *Trainspotting* from Variety Club of Great Britain, London Critics' Circle, and BAFTA Scotland; wins Best Actor from Evening Standard Awards, British Film Institute (award shared with Sir Ian McKellen); wins Best British Actor at *Empire Magazine* Awards; nominated for Emmy Award for guest performance on *ER*.
1998	Wins Best British Actor at *Empire Magazine* Awards.
1999	Becomes well-known in the United States for his role in *Star Wars: Episode I—The Phantom Menace*.

FILMOGRAPHY

1993	Being Human
1994	Shallow Grave
1995	Blue Juice
1996	Brassed Off
	Emma
	The Pillow Book
	Trainspotting
1997	A Life Less Ordinary
	The Serpent's Kiss
1998	Little Voice
	Nightwatch
	Velvet Goldmine
1999	Eye of the Beholder
	Rogue Trader
	Star Wars: Episode I—The Phantom Menace

To Be Released

Nora
Moulin Rouge
Star Wars: Episode II
Star Wars: Episode III

FURTHER READING

Adams, Billy. *Ewan McGregor: The Unauthorized Biography.* New York: Overlook Press, 1999.

Bouzereau, Laurent and Jody Duncan. *Star Wars: The Making of Episode I.* New York: Ballantine Books, 1999.

Brooks, Terry. *Star Wars: Episode I—The Phantom Menace.* New York: Ballantine Books, 1999.

Hatfield, James. *Ewan McGregor: Rising to the Stars.* New York: Berkley Boulevard Books, 1999.

Nickson, Chris. *Ewan McGregor.* New York: St. Martin's Press, 1999.

Pourroy, Janine. *Shooting Star: The Ewan McGregor Story.* New York: Ballantine Books, 1998.

Website

www.ewanspotting.com

ABOUT THE AUTHOR

Award-winning writer VEDA BOYD JONES enjoys the challenge of writing for a variety of readers. Her published works include nine adult novels, four children's historical novels, seven children's biographies, a coloring book, a tiny picture book, and numerous articles and short stories in national magazines. In addition to working at her computer, she teaches writing and speaks at writers' conferences. Mrs. Jones lives in the Missouri Ozarks with her husband, Jimmie. They have three sons, Landon, Morgan, and Marshall.

INDEX